MY BOSS IS ME.

Kike -Lola
Oduoanya

ISBN 978-0-9959974-0-0
Copyright © by Kike-Lola Odusanya | My Boss Is Me.
All Rights Reserved to Aynasudo Publishing

Available online at www.amazon.com

MY BOSS IS ME.

by
Kike-Lola Odusanya

DEDICATION

To my beautiful daughters Adajee & Azaina,
you are and will *always* be my reasons why.

To my mom and step-father, Melrose & Gary Cooley,
this journey would not be possible without your
unrelenting support.

To every woman whose eyes see the pages of this book:
What you want exists; don't stop until you get it.

TABLE OF CONTENTS

Table of Contents

INTRODUCTION

Ｉf you've ever wished you could sit with someone who's been in business for a while and have a deep, real-talk conversation about what it takes to go from having a 9-to-5 to being your own boss, this book is your wish granted.

This unfiltered, series of notes based on real life experiences, gives you insight on everything from ground-up planning to growing your new business to generating enough income to do whatever you want -- to start living the life you've been dreaming of.

I can't honestly say I always knew what I wanted to be when I grew up, or even that I knew I would become my own boss and fall deeply in love with entrepreneurship. All I knew, from the very beginning, was that I was different.

A disobedient spirit, I was called. Rebellious. Never one to accept or believe what I was told, I questioned everything, especially anything I felt was designed to control or confuse me. I'm still that way to this day. I like to come to my own conclusions about how things should be *for me*.

Am I always right? No. Do I always learn? Yes!

After I became an entrepreneur, I realized my unique tendencies and strong personality made me a perfect candidate for life as my own boss.

If you've always felt like the odd one in your circle of friends, embrace it.

Know this: God makes no mistakes. There's a reason you are the way you are. You can leverage your uniqueness to build your empire.

If there's one thing I want you to take from the book, it's this: EVERYTHING IS POSSIBLE! If no one's ever told you this, let me be the first.

Owning your own business doesn't have to remain a dream; it can become your reality. It's absolutely possible. Not just for other people. For you, too.

As soon as you've made up your mind, your mind will go to work creating a path to that reality.

I hope the following glimpse into my story, life lessons, failures and victories provide inspiration and insight for your own journey to live the life you want. Keep grinding.

I wish you nothing but the best and more,
Kike-Lola

I
chapter

MY LIFE BEGAN WHEN IT FELL APART

From as far back as I can remember, my mom said I had to learn things the hard way. Little did I know how true that statement would turn out to be.

It was the summer of 2007, I was 30 years old, and I'd just given birth to my second daughter. I thought I had it all: two beautiful girls, a loving fiance, a fledgling business, a beautiful home, and a steady 9-to-5 job that gave me a comfortable existence.

Within weeks it all came crashing down. I suffered a serious medical emergency that left me in excruciating pain, immobilized, and dependent upon family and friends to care for my most intimate needs and for my new baby.

A month earlier, I was dreaming of how my new business would take off, making me a millionaire and giving my family everything we'd ever dreamed of.

Suddenly, I was in a fight for my life. I spent my days high on painkillers, literally living on my living room couch. I couldn't move without the assistance of a rented walker, and I had to be carried to the main floor powder room that had been adjusted to fit my new condition. It was where I took sponge baths with a watering can while I sat on the toilet, since I was unable to make it up the stairs to the bathroom in my master ensuite.

Along with visiting nurses and aides, my fiance's mom was there around the clock, and she took *amazing* care of me and my baby.

11

She cooked, cleaned, and made sure I had my medications. I'll always be eternally grateful to her for the time she devoted to my recovery.

While my would-be mother-in-law was taking wonderful care of me and her new granddaughter, my relationship with her son was crumbling. Having caretakers in our home, dealing with a newborn and the effects of my total immobility put a serious strain on our relationship.

Even before I was rendered immobile and relegated to a couch existence, our relationship already faced challenges. I was young and naive when we got together, and I allowed love to blind me to things in our relationship that I should never have tolerated.

But this new situation we found ourselves in eventually became the straw that broke the camel's back. Not even two months after I got sick, my fiance decided it was okay for him to spend the night outside of our home ... and just like that, our 11-year relationship was over.

Don't misunderstand, please. My ex is a good man and an amazing father. We were both young, and he just wasn't ready for the type of commitment I deserved. I give him credit; he did a lot more than most men his age would have done. Good people sometimes do bad things. We're still friends today.

So there I was. Alone with two children to provide for, a house that I couldn't afford on my own, a canceled wedding that had been announced to my friends and family, and deposits on the caterer, custom stationery, save-the-dates, invitations and the reception venue.

And yet, none of this was the worst part. What was? The thought of having to return to a job I *absolutely hated*.

I became obsessed, consumed even, with figuring out how to avoid returning to my 9-to-5.

At the time, I had no explanation for why my life had taken such a painful turn, but now I know that our darkest moments prepare us for our brightest days.

There's something that happens when you come face-to-face with the fact that your time here on Earth is limited. That realization has a way of shaking you up --forcing you to move unapologetically in the direction you would go if you had no time to waste.

2

chapter

──────────

NO OBSTACLE IS TOO BIG TO OVERCOME

E verything that takes place in your life — the good, bad and the ugly — is all part of God's master plan.

I had big dreams and, more importantly, bigger plans. I thought that I was going to make it big as a plus-size clothing designer and rip BET's runway alongside labels like Monif C. (who now happens to be an industry legend), but getting sick and not being able to move around changed all that.

My orders fell behind. The last inventory order I placed with a manufacturer in China came back and the sizes were all off. I had taken out a huge loan so I'd have the capital to take my clothing line to the next level, because, truth be told, even before I got sick I had no intention of going back to my job. In fact, the minute I realized I was pregnant I had started to plan my exit.

But being sick made me second guess whether I could make it without returning to work after my maternity leave. The doubts started to kick in. Would it be more responsible for me to just go back to a consistent paycheck? How else would I support myself and my children? How could I afford my house?!

Despite the doubts, I couldn't get over how much I despised my J-O-B. How it literally made me sick. How at that point in my life it was the one thing I knew for sure I *didn't* want. And how I couldn't stand the idea of working for the boss I had at the time - he was a Grade A you-know-what. Looking back now, I'm so thankful for him and his ways.

After calling off the wedding, I focused on my healing. And I made the commitment that I was never going to return to my job.

The first task was to dig myself out of the debt I had incurred from my plus-size clothing business.

Since I was stuck on the couch anyway, I used the down-time to study for my insurance license. I spent 18 months as an insurance agent and financial service professional with World Financial Group. It was hard. I didn't make much money. Truth was I wasn't very good at it; that line of work really wasn't for me.

In 2009 the right opportunity came my way, my time working with WFG prepared me to cease it with confidence. I went on to become a professional in the network marketing industry, but this time in the health and wellness sector. Suddenly, I was traveling to places I'd never been, making an incredible income and honing my skills as an entrepreneur.

I may not have made much money in those first 18 months but I was learning how to be a boss. When the right opportunity presented itself I was ready.

Being an entrepreneur is like getting up every day and going to the amusement park, getting on a bunch of rides, then going home.

Bumps in the road are inevitable, but my hope is that with this book you'll be able to avoid some of the potholes I landed in.

There's no straight line to success, but learning from someone else's mistakes can save you time, frustration, heartache, struggle and money.

Why did I tell you all this? Because I want you to understand that no matter your challenges, you can use them to propel yourself into the life and business you really want. My story doesn't sound like the perfect preparation for becoming a full-time entrepreneur. But that's the point: No one's story is perfect. Yours won't be, either. But like me, you can persevere.

In the pages ahead are the things I wish someone had told me about what it takes to be a successful entrepreneur. You'll find real-talk advice, tips and examples that will allow you to say one day, "My Boss Is Me."

3
chapter

BEFORE YOU QUIT
YOUR JOB

"A goal without a plan is just a wish."

Boss Note: Retrain Your Brain

Here's the thing. We're all conditioned.

It starts the moment we hit kindergarten. Instead of teaching us how to be more of what we innately *are*, the school system trains us to be more of what it wants us to be: good, law abiding citizens who can follow the rules and respond well when instructed ... in other words, great employees.

In school, we're taught to listen to our teachers. We're graded on our ability to take direction, and we're encouraged to follow exact instructions and not to think outside the box or color outside the lines.

Unless your parents or the people who've raised you are unconventional, against-the-grain types, it's likely your conditioning runs deep.

At 18, I was introduced to what I would later learn was "personal development." Intrigued by the late-night infomercial claims about how Tony Robbins' "Personal Power" program had changed people's lives, I ordered it with my very first credit card I got while in college.

That's when I started to retrain my brain. Growing up, my father had done a good job of encouraging me to always think for myself, but Robbins' program started the process of unlearning things that didn't serve me.

Before you even think about starting a business (never mind quitting your 9-to-5) I strongly suggest you start investing in a healthy new mindset. A BOSS mindset. An entrepreneurial one.

Let's flesh out the difference.

When you work for someone, there's a sense of expectation that comes along with being an employee. You invest your time, energy, and expertise. In exchange, your employer owes you wages, perhaps some health benefits, and a maybe a couple of weeks' vacation. Lucky employees also receive some respect, a pat on the back, and the sporadic raise.

When you work for yourself, all those expectations fall squarely on your own shoulders. Want a raise? Find a way to make more money. Want respect and appreciation? Make a product or service that changes people's lives. Want more vacation time? Build a business that can run without your constant presence.

Entrepreneurs eat what they kill and spend what they earn. Everything you gain is a result of your own efforts, so you need to push yourself and tap into the deeper reasons *why* you do what you do.

As an entrepreneur, your thoughts about money and your ability to determine how and how much you make will change. You'll start thinking about the bottom line - quite literally, the number that's left when you add up your income and subtract your expenses. The number you arrive at is the bottom line.

Entrepreneurs see investments in their own skills and knowledge as an investment in their business and themselves. They don't feel sorry for themselves or make excuses; they see a challenge and create a solution. Entrepreneurs don't feel entitled. They go out and get what they want. Period.

Entrepreneurs don't wait to be told, they tell themselves and others what to do.

Entrepreneurs are secure about the value they offer and can confidently communicate that value not only to others but to themselves!

Finally, entrepreneurs immerse themselves in all things related to financial improvement. Seek wisdom in this area. Read classic finance books and the biographies of financially successful people.

Know this: The only difference between you and the entrepreneurs you admire is time, knowledge and effort. You can create a dream life and wealth, too. Making money is not a secret in a club that you're shut out of. It's open to anyone and everyone. Knowing this will free you of self doubt and limiting beliefs

Boss Note: Have a Plan. Be Strategic.

My decision to quit my job came suddenly. My mom was convinced I was suffering from postpartum depression. Trust and believe she had the whole church praying for me.

When I left my job, I had no plan. No money. No guidance. I risked everything. I wasted a lot of time, money, and cried many tears. I now see how with a plan,

things could have been so much smoother, not just for me ... but for my girls, too. As I grew as a business owner, my daughters were growing, too; they were there each step of the way.

The type of plan I'm talking about is *more* than a traditional business plan. What I needed and what I strongly recommend you start with is a strategic plan.

A strategic plan identifies the best-case scenario for your dream life and business, allowing you to reverse-engineer to discover what steps are needed to take you from where you are now to where you want to go.

There are so many ways to approach running a business and so many businesses you can run. But it's essential to know your goal. Be clear about your idea, how you will generate an income, what impact you will make and the lifestyle you want to have. This knowledge gives you clarity and power.

When you have no plan and no strategy, you'll get caught up in a swirl of saying "yes" to everything, sowing seeds everywhere, wearing yourself thin and running around dissipating your impact and squandering your energy. Clarity lets you know when to say "no" and keeps you focused on your goals.

The more specific you are about what you want, the more easily your brain will be able to problem-solve your path.

Know what you're aiming for. A fuzzy target is hard to hit.

What problem do you want your business to solve? For whom? Do you want to work solo, or with a team? From an office in your home or outside your home? Do you want to travel all the time? How much money do you want to make? Whom would you like to influence? In what way? How will you deliver value? How will you build a relationship with your ideal customer? How do you want to *feel*, running your business?

You don't need to answer these questions all at once. But you do need to answer them. When you do, you'll have the only business plan you'll ever need. It'll be all encompassing, specific and will allow you to think through the steps needed to reach every goal.

> **Boss Note: Plan Your Dream Business Around Your Dream Life**

When I started as an entrepreneur, I spent most of my time on the go. My network marketing business took me to the homes of potential clients and business partners, usually in the evenings and on the weekends when they were off work.

Home parties are the heart of network marketing. At the height of my career, I would lead as many as 14 home parties in one weekend. On Thursday nights I held weekly meetings that rotated among hotels in various parts of my city. While I was running around, I went through four nannies and missed out on precious time with my girls. Obviously, I knew nothing about Life Planning.

When I was introduced to the concept, I couldn't believe how intuitive it was, and I wondered why I'd never thought of it. Life Planning doesn't need to be complicated. Just take a few hours or days and write down what you really want, not only your business goals, but goals for family life, health, your spirit, and your leisure time.

You'd be surprised how easy it is to choose the right path for your business when you have the blueprint of the lifestyle you want, to test each option against. For example, if you know you need alone time to recharge and hate the idea of working seven days a week, then opening a retail business (where consistent hours and customer interaction are critical) isn't the right business for you.

For me, it's important that I'm able to put my daughter on the school bus, make her a warm breakfast and be available to go to her school to pick her up or attend an event. I made this a priority later on in my career, as I developed the need to build a business flexible enough for me to spend lots of time with my girls.

When my youngest daughter is grown, my dream life — and therefore, my dream job — may change. It's okay to adapt and evolve. It's okay to be multi-passionate. Not everyone has their life and career mapped out in kindergarten. Allow your story to unfold and if a new season in your business proves to be fruitful, wanted and rewarding, go for it.

If you have the luxury of creating (or even just deciding on) the lifestyle you want to have *before* you start your business, do it! It'll set you up to have freedom as an entrepreneur, rather than being a slave to the business you started. After all true freedom is what you're looking for, isn't it?

4
chapter

STARTING SMART

*"If you wouldn't buy what you're selling,
no one else will, either."*

Boss Note: Become a Student of Marketing

One of the things women are great at ... and often spend too much time doing, is making everything pretty (and just 'making' in general.)

Lots of women entrepreneurs spend more time creating beautiful logos and color-matching branded websites than they do thinking through actual marketing strategy. Trust me, I know what I'm talking about; I've done it, too. Women spend a ton of time making their businesses beautiful in the mistaken belief that pretty visuals equal great offerings and/or marketing. If it looks beautiful, how could someone *not* buy? Right?! Wrong.

In the network marketing industry (where I cut my teeth when I was starting out) there are three key elements to success:

1. A great product to sell

2. A great compensation plan

3. A powerful marketing strategy

Marketing is simply introducing your business to as many potential customers as you can - giving them the opportunity to see how you and your product or service would add value to their lives, and ultimately giving them the opportunity to purchase from you.

Great marketing is about being visible and memorable. Remember the old saying, "out of sight, out of mind?" You know your marketing has been successful when you're the first thing to pop into someone's head when they think of a certain thing, color, product, and/or service.

Some examples of marketing strategies you might use for your business:

- If you're a clothing or jewelry designer: Sending your clothes or jewelry to a fashion blogger who'll mention what she's wearing and link back to your store in her blog post or social media.

- If you're a cupcake maker: Booking a gig catering desserts for a bridal show. Not only will you get paid for the event, but you'll be able to market your business with signs and postcards so that future brides can keep you in mind for their weddings.

- If you're a childcare provider: Offering your current clients discounted or bonus hours of care when they refer a friend.

- If you're a musician: Teaming up with a local charity for a benefit concert. They'll excitedly promote you to everyone on their mailing list and community when they spread the word about the event, since they will benefit, too.

- If you're an accountant: Writing guest blog posts full of helpful financial advice and linking back to your site. Or guesting on a podcast and sharing some of your wisdom. Or offering free printable budgeting worksheets on your website for visitors to download, so before they ever purchase from you, you've added value to their lives.

- If you're a product-based business: Starting and running a Facebook ad campaign targeting your target market

- If you sell online programs or coaching: Putting on a free webinar where you teach attendees something *really* valuable, introducing them to the wisdom you have to share and at the end, how else they can work with you.

If you're not sure where to start with your company's marketing strategy, read all the posts and books you can by bloggers and entrepreneurs who have mastered the art of marketing. You can start by visiting www.mybossisme.co/blog

Boss Note: Make Money for Your Business BEFORE You Borrow From the Bank.

In 2002, I started a plus size clothing business. At that time, I started out with extra dollars from my paycheques and some money from my saving and then eventually I decided to get a $20,000 line of credit.

Investing in your business is always a good idea, but I made some costly mistakes I literally had to pay for.

Mistakes like:

- Spending too much on things like websites, pattern-making and samples

- Spending indiscriminately rather than being resourceful

- Failing to budget or keep detailed records of money spent

- Failing to research as much as I could have, such as asking other business owners what was worth investing in and what wasn't

- Deciding I needed *more* money ... and taking out an even bigger loan

If I could do it all again, I wouldn't have taken the bigger loan. If I started from scratch today, I would have:

- Researched every purchase thoroughly to make sure I got the best deal, of the best quality that would make the biggest impact on my business

- Taken the time to map out a budget and stick to it as much as possible, diligently tracking where money was going and coming from

- Focused on reinvesting profit (as much as possible) back into the business until I created the funds necessary to grow

- Been a lot more frugal with the money I had - now-a-days I *think* a lot more and *spend* a lot less

- Thought about ways to make more money instead of borrowing it

You've got to learn to stretch a dollar as an entrepreneur. Instead of throwing money around, you've got to be smart, strategic and respectful of the cash you have.

Money is a lot like water. You need it to live, but too much can be dangerous.

As Peter Drucker (whose writings contributed to the culture of modern corporations) says,

"You can't manage what you don't measure."

Boss Note: Test it Before You Invest in It.

Use the resources you already have to create what you want to share with the world. Then begin to sell that thing (or even other things, for that matter) to generate the money you need to invest in your business, instead of heading straight to the bank for a loan or looking for grants or other sources of free money.

When you start with your own capital, you're able to test the market. You can observe what your customers purchase most and adapt your strategy accordingly, without the pressure of a huge loan hanging over your head.

If you're not great with money, invest in learning about it. The internet is full of financial education resources for entrepreneurs, and they're 100 percent free. Google and YouTube University are real. Read books on financial literacy or if you're really ready to get set up right, book an appointment with an accountant to work through your numbers.

Mismanagement of money can kill your business quickly and leave you bankrupt. Thinking about finances may not feel like the sexiest way to spend your time, but take it from me, you'll start to feel super sexy when the money starts rolling in and piling up.

I thought borrowing wouldn't be a problem, especially since I was incorporated. I thought the money I owed should anything happen would be owed by my company and not me personally. But due to the way I incorporated and the bank's inability to seize the type of assets they deemed valuable, it didn't exactly work that way.

I recommend large business loans *only* if you have no other alternative or if your project requires some sort of costly initial purchase.

It never ceases to amaze me how many people contact me asking for guidance on how to obtain a grant.

Many new entrepreneurs will launch a business and immediately look for a grant, before they've even put skin in the game themselves. Put yourself in an investor's shoes. What kind of track record and characteristics would you look for in a business owner?

The best way to proceed when you've launched a business is to research your idea and market and then test it before investing substantial amounts of time or money. If your idea is commercially viable, your clients or the people you serve will let you know! Don't be afraid to put your idea to the test. And don't forget to collect feedback from your customers or clients. That's how you grow and improve not only your product or service, but also your customer experience and your business' reputation in a good way.

Boss Note: Structure is Important. You Need It to Survive.

I remember the ecstatic feeling I had when I became self-employed for the first time … knowing that I didn't ever have to report to anyone or deal with rush hour traffic ever again. I was like a kid in a candy store.

As time went on, my days quickly ran into nights and my nights quickly ran into days, which led to weeks running into months. I wasn't accomplishing half the things I needed to do.

I had zero structure and I lost sight of the fact that now that I had no boss, I'd have to work even harder than I did at my day job. All the inspiration and discipline had to come from me.

To ensure you have some structure, here's what you can do.

Write a job description for yourself as an entrepreneur. What are your responsibilities? Then make yourself do them. As your own boss, you'll need to tell yourself what to do, otherwise you'll end up doing a whole lot of nothing.

Learning how to manage your time effectively is paramount. I put God, family and income-generating activities at the top of the list (in that order) then add everything else, prioritizing tasks that require the least effort and create the most impact.

It's so easy to fall victim to structureless days. Days where you have *no idea* how your time was spent or where the hours went. Days when you are frustrated with the fact that you achieved very little. It's okay to have what I call "waste days" sometimes, but they should be far fewer than your productive ones.

Having a simple schedule is all it takes.

I like to use timers while I'm working. The "Pomodoro Method" works really well. Here's how to use timers to improve your workflow:

1. Set a timer for 25 or 30 minutes and spend that time intensely focused and dedicated to one task. Close every other tab on your computer. Put away any devices you're not using. Put your phone on airplane mode and turn on some instrumental music if you need a little background noise (instrumental is best so you don't get distracted by the words to the song and start singing along). Once you have everything set up, get to work!

2. When the timer goes off, set the timer for five minutes and reward yourself with a short, guilt-free break to do whatever mindless activity you want.

3. When that timer goes off, set it again for 25 or 30 minutes and get back to work.

You'll be amazed at how much you get done and how little time you waste.

When you make your schedule for the day, don't forget to take *all* of your needs into account - not just your business needs. Schedule time to pray, meditate, move your body or work on self development, schedule time to spend with friends, spouse or significant other. All time should be accounted for.

In my early stages of entrepreneurship, I tried many expert-recommended methods of planning my day. I bought planners, systems and schedulers, but they never worked for me.

What I do now is simply divide my day into sections:

- The first few hours are dedicated to myself. Those hours consist of prayer and quiet time for mini-meditation. I listen to personal development books and podcasts and try to go for a walk.

If you're a person who works out, the morning is the perfect time.

- Then I have to have a few hours to get my daughter ready for school. I actually write that time with her into the schedule as well!

- From 9 a.m. to noon, I focus on income-generating activities. That might look like creating a plan for a coaching session or following up with potential clients. Marketing, sales and promotion fall into this window of time too.

- I schedule an hour for lunch from noon to 1pm. It's so easy to keep going and going and run myself ragged. This break at lunchtime helps me come back to work with a clear, more focused mind.

- From 1 to 4, I focus on all the other elements that keep a business running and growing. These hours are usually filled with responding to emails and reaching out to people I need to touch base with.

The secret to making this time-blocking method work for you is to write what's going to happen in each block of time. That way, your time won't be spent planning what to do or sifting through your inbox, jumping at whatever feels most immediate.

On another note, you hear a lot today about work/life balance. As far as I'm concerned, the idea of balance is an illusion. It all comes down to prioritizing things that will keep you sane. Schedule them and make those things non-negotiables. That's how you maintain sanity. It's really that simple.

I can't provide you with an exact, no fail step by step plan; no one can. Such a thing doesn't exist. People will always try to sell you on what they did and what worked for them but it doesn't mean it will work for you too. There's no one way to run your business. You're the only one who can figure out through trial and error what works for you and what doesn't.

"The less you say, the more you get done. When you move in silence, your efforts will eventually speak for themselves."

Boss Note: Talk Less, Do More.

There are a number of reasons new entrepreneurs sometimes feel the need to share what they're doing. Sometimes it's pure excitement. Sometimes you're seeking validation. Sometimes you want feedback or clarity.

Whatever the reason, before you share, step back and think about your motives. Remember, you're the one with the vision. You're the one who needs to know in your heart that it's going to work, no matter what others may think.

If you're going to share or ask for advice, be mindful about who you ask.

Choose people who are able to give you valid, practical advice based on experience, and not just opinion. Asking people who are not likeminded for advice, or sharing your exciting new plans with the wrong person, can cause you to be unnecessarily distracted, derailed, discouraged, or worse, maybe even quit.

Seek out someone who's been there. Talk to someone whose results you admire. And don't be deflated if you don't get affirmation from someone you expected to be encouraged by. When you're confident of the value you can deliver, and when you begin to build up a library of small victories, making customers and clients happy, affirmation from others will begin to matter to you less and less.

The secret is less talking and more doing. Let your actions speak for themselves. There's nothing worse than the woman who talks for years about launching a business but never even gets as far as making a website.

Everyone has to respect the person who's been quietly and diligently working and launches *something*. Even if it doesn't work out the way they wanted it to, they've already done more than most people.

Motivation that comes from within as a result of witnessing your own successes is a beautiful, beautiful thing. Focus on making your first $5,000 or $10,000. That will help you build all the belief that you need in yourself and what you're offering.

Boss Note: No One Makes It Without a Little Help.

If I had gotten a coach (or even knew coaches existed!) when I was starting out, I would have invested in one much earlier. While it may seem like a trendy or even ultra fancy thing to do, there are practical reasons to hire a coach.

In launching a business, you're likely doing something you've never done before. It's important that you maximize your energy, passion and drive by channeling it correctly into the actions that'll make a big impact on your business, rather than wasting energy aimlessly sifting through blog after blog and webinar after webinar to patch together your own strategy from disjointed free resources that never give you 100 percent of the information.

Just like an elite athlete or famous singer, having a coach helps you improve. Maybe your business is going great. You've had a great launch or your products are really starting to sell. You may feel like you've got a good thing going. And it may be true. But that's all the more reason to invest in coaching. Coaching is about taking your business from good to great. Coaching is what takes a talented athlete and turns her into an Olympic gold medalist. Because as you grow and improve and go to new levels in business, your competition will become those businesses that are at the next level already, and in order to succeed there, you'll need the edge and insights a coach can provide.

Coaching is rarely about learning new information (although with a good coach, you will). Coaching is designed to take you from where you are to where you want to go with speed.

A coach will hold you accountable and stretch you beyond your comfort zone. It's hard to boss ourselves around. A coach is someone you hire to keep you from sliding backward into over-thinking and overwhelm, they will help to move you forward.

Investing in a coach has been the best decisions I've made in my business. My first business coach, Tony Robbins, has a mantra I've been using since I was 18: "constant and never-ending improvement" or "CANI" for short. It's important that you're always finding ways to do better and be better, especially in business.

So let's say you're ready to find a coach to help take your business to the next level - or get it off the ground. How do you find a good one? I've spent thousands of dollars on coaching and personal development over the years and I've learned a few things about how to hire the right person. Here are my recommendations:

- Stalk them first (in a benign way, of course)! Start watching what they do on a daily basis. Are they consistent? Do they offer value? Does their approach resonate with you? Are their other clients experiencing gains and wins in their businesses? Is their free content (blog, newsletter, social media posts) worthwhile and insightful?

- If you're still not sure about whether to work together, start with an entry-level investment, like an e-book or e-course before you shell out hundreds or thousands of dollars on a one-on-one coaching package.

- Attend a workshop, webinar, weekend mastermind or group coaching session. Again, this in-person/virtually in-person interaction is going to give you a good idea of whether you're a good fit for each other.

- Ask the right questions before you pay, like what topics they can work with you on, the level of access and contact you'll have, the length and frequency of sessions, what kind of follow-up or accountability they offer, etc.

Don't be afraid to tell a potential coach what you want and need. If they can't provide you with it, don't settle. They are not the coach for you. To learn more about how a coach can help you, I can be reached at www.mybossisme.co/contact

Boss Note: Never Take Criticism from Someone Who Isn't Where You Want To Be.

Now that you know why you need a coach, it's important that you also understand why you need to find a mentor and what the difference is.

You may be thinking, "Why have a mentor when I already have a coach? Aren't they the same thing?"

While there is some overlap, a coach is someone you hire to help you get from Point A to Point B in the smartest, most profitable way. A mentor is who you look to to determine what your Point B even is. A mentor should also have a successful business or career - preferably one that you would aspire to have. They've already experienced the victories you're looking forward to.

A mentor models best practices. They're generous with their wisdom and they can draw from their rich experiences to help you make better informed decisions.

Chances are, your mentor isn't someone who's in your inner circle, or even someone you know personally.

I've never met most of the people I consider to be my mentors. I've been following, studying and learning from many people for years, through their books, courses, videos, etc. You'd be surprised by how much you can learn from people you've never met.

If you're looking for a mentor to meet with in person though, a simple way to get one is to focus first on building a genuine relationship with that person. Find a way to be in their presence or approach them via email. Let them know how you can help them, before you ask for help. If you get a chance to be around the right person, you'll most likely get everything you need or are looking for.

Remember, successful people can afford to get their own coffee, breakfast or dinner. While it doesn't hurt to attempt to take someone out to grab a bite to eat, you'll most likely have a better chance of being able to receive the mentoring you want if you come up with something more creative or beneficial to the person you hope will mentor you.

If you get the opportunity to spend time with the person, show up prepared with great questions and be a good listener. But ONLY after you've attempted to help them first. Successful people are always being asked for something by someone. Be the breath of fresh air and change the script. If a connection is made, be sure to stay in touch. Once you've made that connection, you can keep the relationship going.

5

chapter

_____

BUILD THE BUSINESS; BUILD YOURSELF

Boss Note: A Great Business Is Built With Love

There was a time while I was building my second network marketing business that I admittedly let my ego get the best of me.

I was coming in contact with so many people and making more money than I ever dreamt possible, I wasn't always as nice to people as I could have been. One of my close friends had become my assistant. She was with me everywhere I went. One day, somebody complained to her mom, who was also in the same business with us, about something rude that I'd said to her. Looking back, I sometimes shake my head. I can't even believe some of the things I said and did.

But graciously, my friend's mom took the opportunity to offer me some advice (instead of scolding me or writing me off all together.) She said, "Kike, this business needs to be built with love."

Think about what Love is; Love is patient. Love is kind. Love is enduring. Love doesn't show favoritism. If you really stop to think about it, love really should permeate the fabric of your business. It should influence the way you treat the people you serve and come in contact with every day. I didn't fully understand everything she was saying at the time. I mean, I knew I was wrong, but the lesson didn't fully sink in until later. Nowadays I focus on treating everyone I come in contact with, for business and in my personal life, the way I would want to be treated. Always remember how you want and like to be treated. Treat others the same way. This advice is so simple, yet so profound.

Boss Note: Go Deep, Not Wide

When you become clear about exactly what it is that you want to achieve as a business owner or self-employed person, the things you spend time mastering should be in line with your focus.

For example, if you want to become a speaker and author, then you need to focus all of your efforts on mastering those areas. As a speaker, you should be figuring out: how to command an audience, how to tell stories, how to change the sound and pitch of your voice to move the people who are listening, and how structure of a great speech.

As an author, you should read great writing. Classic writing. Take writing classes, if you feel the need to. Have others edit your work. You should study sentence structure, story structure, essay writing and what it means to convey your thoughts in a beautiful, digestible and actionable way. Then, most importantly, you should practice. Once you become a good writer, you may need to research what goes into self-publishing and what steps to take first.

Read the key blogs for your industry. Find podcasts that your customers love and figure out why. Read the biographies of successful business people. Take a class at the local university. Go to conferences. Join an entrepreneur MeetUp group. Take an online course.

When you take in a steady stream of wisdom, you'll expand your own creative and problem-solving abilities, giving yourself an edge in your business and the ability to see both the details and the big picture.

When you're going it alone as an entrepreneur, you don't have to be limited to your own thoughts and ideas. Get Google-ing.

Also take the time to learn how you learn. Do you need to hear the material? See a visual presentation? Test out the new skill yourself?

But be mindful not to become obsessed with consuming without executing. Knowledge is only powerful if you put what you've learned into action.

It's easy to become inundated with personal development and the next expert guru. You can fall into the trap of wanting to be good at everything. But people who are rewarded with profitable businesses are often those who go deep on a subject and master it, rather than trying to tackle everything.

Because when you go deep, and learn to do one thing or just a few things really well, you'll have something to share that's not readily available, something beyond so much of the surface level stuff available these days.

You'll have mastery. That makes what you have to offer valuable. That makes *you* valuable.

Go the extra mile in your field. Study more. Read more. Ask more questions. Learn more. Practice more. You'll end up becoming the best or at least that's what you should be striving for.

Boss Note: Know Your Target Market

All business is about people. You sell to people. You serve people. You solve people's problems. You disappoint people. You delight people. You confuse people. You convince people. People are the ones recommending you to their friends. People are the ones sharing your Facebook statuses and responding to or writing you emails. People are the ones giving you their money and their trust.

When you think of business as bringing value to people, you'll be so much more successful than everyone who thinks business is about telling their own story, building their own empire or having something to feel proud of.

Figure out who your target market is and study them. Think of it like meeting someone for the first time and then gradually getting to know them, then becoming life long friends.

The process of figuring out and getting to know your target market intimately evolves over time, once you have a general idea of who they are, what they like, where they go and what they do, it then becomes your job to get to know them the way you do your best friend or even yourself.

Do you need help discovering your target market? Download a free guide, 7 Steps to Quitting Your Job Like a Boss. Visit www.mybossisme.co/quityourjob

Boss Note: Know Thy Self

Do you know your strengths as a business owner? What are your skills? What are you talented at doing? What does everyone always thank you for doing or being in their lives?

Self awareness is indispensable when you become your own boss. No one's going to sit you down and do an end-of-the-year evaluation, working through every way that you've grown and succeeded that year. As your own boss, you'll have to do that yourself.

A lack of self awareness could mean that you're stunting the growth of your business without even knowing it.

Knowing yourself also helps you set goals and make decisions more wisely.

For example, an extrovert might not flourish in a work-from-home environment. They may not be taking into account the fact that they'll be home alone all day without any office friends or people to talk to.

I strongly suggest that you read the book *StrengthsFinder* by Tom Rath. It'll help you get to know which one of your traits you can leverage to launch and grow your successful business.

Boss Note: Promote Yourself. Hard.

If you don't promote yourself and your business who will?

If you're in business, promotion is part of the process. Promote your business until you feel sick of yourself, and start to wonder if you're doing too much and then go at it a little bit harder.

You're competing to be seen with companies that have mega-dollars to get themselves in front of the same people that you want to be seen by.

Don't worry about what others say and whether you're "doing too much." If they're talking, you're on the right path. Keep going hard for you and yours.

When "ish: hits the fan, which it will from time to time, the same people you're worrying about now most likely won't be there for you.

Do what you have to do to secure your finances and your future for you and yours. Those talking about you now someday will be telling people that they "knew you when."

Boss Note: Acknowledge That You Are Not Your Past

I had my first child earlier than some people said I should have. Becoming a mom in my late teens was a crash course in real-world *everything*. It forced me to focus, helped me to develop an inner strength, and brought on a whole lot of realizations about life and the life I wanted my daughter to live, much sooner than I would have had them, if not for becoming a mom at 17.

Looking back, I'm not sure what even made me think that becoming a mom at such a young age was even okay. It's something that I oftentimes think about now that I'm older.

My decision to give my daughter life cost me many things. My childhood was cut short. I never really got a chance to get to know myself until later on in life, because I never had the time to think about anything but providing the best for my daughter. It also cost me a relationship with the first man I ever loved - my Dad.

Becoming a teen mom is one thing, but becoming a teen mom when your father is Yoruba Nigerian man is a another situation entirely. Even though I turned out pretty well, I don't think he ever got over the hurt, disappointment and shame. Our relationship hasn't been the same since.

None of us can change our past, but we can learn and grow from it. Sure, I made mistakes, but they made me who and what I am today.

Without the determination to make the best life I could for my daughters, I wouldn't be where I am today, and I wouldn't change that for the world.

6

chapter

YOU'RE ON YOUR WAY: TIME FOR A PEP TALK

"Fear is the betrayer of the future you deserve.
If you allow it to, it will stop you and keep you
right where you are."

Boss Note: Whatever It Is, You Can Do It

When I started out in business, I was deathly afraid to speak in front of others. I could barely introduce myself to people I'd see at meetings twice a week, every week, let alone speak in front of a crowd of strangers. I remember winning an award for the being the top Recruiter of the Month while in the insurance industry. I was asked to share a few words about how I was able to achieve what I did. I was terrified, barely got any sleep the night before and when I finally hit the stage, my hands were shaking so badly that I could barely hold the microphone still enough to talk into it.

Needless to say, this is no longer a huge problem for me, don't get me wrong I still get nervous if I have to address a crowd but I'm able to manage my fears a lot better now. I want to take every opportunity I can to share my story to help others achieve the kind of success I have enjoyed. In order to do that I can not allow fear to prevent me from ultimately helping others.

The journey from scared to confident requires ongoing work. I had to learn to overcome a lack of confidence, a penchant for worry, and the fear of failure. What I learned along the way is that the strength of my convictions and my faith in God and in myself were all I needed to carry me over the finish line.

When I started out as entrepreneur, I passed up too many opportunities because of fear. I was afraid to speak in front of audiences. I was afraid to do interviews. I was afraid of so many things.

I always thought that maybe I wasn't good enough, articulate enough, smart enough or that I'd freeze up or say the wrong thing. The reality is we are all enough and need to start somewhere in order to get better.

"When an opportunity in line with your goals presents itself, say yes and figure out how to make it happen."

Now, I'm not advocating putting yourself in a situation that's out of the realm of everything you know. Don't try to speak intelligently about a topic you don't understand or have no knowledge of. I'm talking about times when you're perfectly equipped or even somewhat equipped to do what's being asked, but fear of embarrassment or self consciousness or unworthiness keeps you from saying yes.

Understand this: Fear is simply a result of facing the unknown.

It's so important that you feel the fear and do it anyway. Don't wait for some mystical confidence to arrive at your doorstep. You'll only get more confident as you make a conscious effort to do the thing that scares you until it is no longer scary (or less scary at least). Action is the only real cure for fear.

Reframe how you think of fear. A friend of mine says, "Fear is an acronym for: Face Everything And Rise." If you face it, it can elevate who and where you are.

In my life as an entrepreneur, I've spent way too much time worrying. I've obsessed about "what if" and the "how" and a million other things I have *zero* control over.

Worry wastes time. It's bad for your business and it's even worse for your health.

I truly believe that If something is meant to be, it'll be. That doesn't mean it will happen by magic. But if you're putting in the work, have a good idea and a sound plan, have faith.

Milestones may not be happening as quickly as you'd like, but stay focused and carry on. Reward yourself for the effort, not just results.

That means if you've sent out 100 sales emails like you wanted to, be proud of that. You've done your part. Worrying about how or whether each of the 100 recipients will respond is a waste of time. You did the thing that you can control and should feel accomplished in that.

If your efforts didn't yield you the results you wanted, don't beat yourself up simply adjust the amount of effort or tweak you strategy and/or plan.

If you ever find yourself in a storm, just do your best and keep pushing, focus on what's is within your power to control. Things will be okay, I promise.

"Every storm eventually runs out of rain."   .

When I look back at the last 10 years, I realize I wasted too much time worrying about things that I had no control over, things that I couldn't fix or that I had no business worrying about. I wish I'd spent time instead on doing, giving and serving.

The next time you feel worried, ask yourself:

- What work can I do toward my goal?
- Whom can I help or serve?

Talk to your customers and ask them about *their* needs. Interact with your following on social media. It'll switch your energy and focus from your own problems onto being the answer to other people's prayers.

Boss Note: Criticism Doesn't Mean You're Doing It Wrong

"Don't tune everything out. Take the meat and spit out the bones."

Until I started my business, I'd never really been in a position to be criticized or talked about, because I'd never done anything out of the ordinary or worth mentioning.

But when you start a business, you're putting yourself out there in a way that leaves you vulnerable to the thoughts and opinions of others. You're asking others to look at what you offer the world. You have to realize people will have an opinion about it.

When the comments and opinions start to roll in, know that some of them will be negative. That's inevitable. Be thankful and get excited. The comments, good or bad, show you've done something worth mentioning. PEOPLE NOTICED YOU!

You've created something that people are emotionally engaged in. Something helpful enough or interesting enough or innovative enough for people to have an opinion about.

You can encourage yourself with the truth that most people spewing hate and jealously online or otherwise are doing it because they've never felt what it's like to put the effort into creating something, so it's easy to be a keyboard gangster from a position of safety.

Not every critique is helpful, but not every critique is worthless. Train yourself to use criticism to get better. Sometimes critics have valid points. Learn to differentiate between the "talkers" and the "doers."

Learn to guard your mind, but open your heart to those worth listening to.

Boss Note: Harness Your Secret Superpower. Yes, You Really Have One.

"Your thoughts control the trajectory of your life and business. You'll go and grow wherever you put your focus."

Most people will sit down and wonder whether certain things are possible. But the only way to really know is to do it, whatever "it" is. Start taking action, small steps towards your goals

If you spend your time wondering if you can achieve your goal, or even doubting that you can, you'll just come up with more reasons to doubt and more reasons why you can't.

When you take the time to write things down, it forces you to become super clear about what you want, which then motivates you to act on the things you need to do.

Once you've written your dreams on paper, break them into bite-sized, tangible goals. Then you'll be able to break those goals down into the smaller actions needed to achieve them and then those small actions become your plan for each day.

Research shows there's something special about putting a pen to paper. It actually triggers your mind to make the things that you've written become a reality!

"Get some goals, write them down, watch shit happen."

Erykah Badu

If you decide in your heart that what you're after is achievable, your mind will go to work to get you there.

The entrepreneurial journey is the most powerful personal development any woman will ever experience. It'll expose strengths, skills and character traits that would never have been uncovered if you weren't challenged in the way that entrepreneurship does - it forces you to stretch past your limits, adapt and grow.

You'll learn the most about your own power to create and to provide for yourself and your family, only once your explore entrepreneurship. You'll watch yourself nurture an idea and then watch it become a reality that you've executed with hard work. Few things in the world can surpass that feeling.

As an entrepreneur, you have no limits, only new levels.

If I had stayed at my 9-to-5, I would have never witnessed my own ability to overcome, excel and do greater things in the way that I have during my time as an entrepreneur.

I firmly believe that you have super powers. Stop wondering and get to work! It's already yours, all you have to do is go get it But don't forget, the real work starts between the ears, you've got to spend the time to improve your state of mind.

Boss Note: Talk Yourself to Success

When I became self-employed, I'd talk to myself *so* much that my children would ask me if I was talking to myself or to them!

I was talking to myself for many reasons, to practice my pitch, become more confident approaching people and telling them about what I do, rewiring my mind by telling myself what I wanted myself to believe and not just what I had always known.

The reality is, talking to yourself is a powerful growth tool. Here are eight reasons why it's important to talk to yourself:

1. Speaking to yourself is a practical way to retrain your mind.

2. Speaking to yourself empowering truths about who you are will boost your confidence.

3. Talking to yourself will give you space to practice expressing things you're not used to expressing. I'd often practice what I wanted to say when I encountered a certain situation, so that I would be able to articulate myself intelligently.

4. It gives you pressure-free space to get good at articulating what you do succinctly. Being able to express the heart of your business and the problem you solve in a quick and memorable way is a skill that'll serve you for the rest of your life. You have to be able to tell people what you do in a few minutes.

5. It helps you to clarify your thoughts.

6. It helps you lay out pros and cons so you can work through a problem.

7. It helps you audit your own thoughts to make sure they're healthy and helpful.

8. It reduces stress! (When you say the right things.)

My favorite form of self-talk is a daily affirmation.

Simply put, affirmations are sentences or phrases you repeat aloud daily. When you speak an affirmation, you're declaring something to be true. All of us speak to ourselves every day. Often we speak the same thoughts over and over for years. Sadly they're not always positive things. Whether good or bad, the things we say affirm the life we live.

When you commit to speaking daily affirmations aloud, you're rewiring your brain to believe the things you said are true, whether they're things about yourself, your business or the world around you.

The more you repeat something, the more your brain will realize that that thing is important to you. When your brain realizes how important something is to you, it'll get busy and actually help you to achieve that thing (your goals).

Some say it takes 21 days of consistent repetition from an affirmation to make a mark on your psyche ... and for you to notice a difference in your everyday life.

If you've been struggling with a particular area of your life and you've never really been able to see yourself as the thing that you are trying to be, you may need to speak your affirmation longer than 21 days. You may need to say it to yourself several times a day.

One of my favorite affirmations is:

> "I am enough; I have everything I need to create everything I desire."

Boss Note: God Is The Plug

"Put God at the center of all you do and you will never ever fail."

No matter your belief system, there will be times in your personal and business life when you will feel the need to put your trust, fears, perhaps your life itself, in the hands of that higher power.

For me, it means recognizing that I didn't create myself - that He's the Creator of the whole universe, including me. And it means acknowledging that and leaning on Him amplifies my power, because He's the source. And that trusting His word amplifies my wisdom, because that's where He's spoken it. It means seeking what *He* wants for my life. Sitting still and tuning in and listening. It means putting His will above my own, rather than using God as a cosmic butler to serve my every request. It means I ask what He would have me do, and do more of that instead. I ask Him to give me the courage, wisdom and increase faith to carry it out.

I believe that when my life is in line with what God wants for me, I will go farther faster and keep what's given to me. He will surpass anything you've ever dreamed.

You'll have true peace knowing it's not up to you to make the world spin; that's someone else's job. I've tried to do it myself before but it didn't work, over the years I've had to learn how to let go and let God do his thing.

7

chapter

———————

WE'RE ALL ON OUR
OWN PATH; YOUR TIME
WILL COME

Boss Note: It's Not a Race. There's No Rush

In the early stages of my business, I constantly felt like I was behind.

I felt like I wasn't doing enough, like my business wasn't growing fast enough. All these self assessments that left me feeling like I'd fallen short happened when I looked at others in my industry and compared their milestones to mine (or lack, thereof).

The reality is, you don't know what's happening behind the scenes. The woman with the most polished website in the world may not have any customers.

The boss lady with the Instagram-perfect lifestyle may be struggling through relationship problems. The one who started a business at the same time as you, who seems to be so much more successful, may have received love money from a rich family member.

Everyone is human. We are all made of flesh and blood. There is no need to be jealous or worship anyone or put anyone above or below you.

Just remember that the legwork, the grind, the blood, sweat and tears taking place behind the scenes will creating the image of success you are after, because that's what it really takes to be successful.

Make it your goal to emulate the effort, not the final result. Emulating the efforts of successful people is what will bring you success — not just rushing to create a perfect looking exterior with no solid foundation upon which to build.

Rushing sometimes takes the form of:

- Planning a big fancy launch party or releasing a shiny looking service, before you've taken the time to test, refine and create an excellent product or service that sells itself

- Obsessing over getting media coverage, recognition and/or Instagram followers because the interviews and big numbers will make you feel better about yourself

- Going forward with plans or products even though it doesn't feel right, because you're afraid of missing out

- Lacking patience and wanting things to happen before their time

If you're rushing, slow down and take the time to build your business on a strong foundation. Invest your time in doing the work. Recognition will come on its own; you don't need to chase it. Anything that God has for you is already yours. There's no need to race and cut corners to get there sooner.

Boss Note: It's Okay To Take a Break Sometimes

Every once in awhile, take time to unplug and do something that's not business-related. You need time to decompress, unwind and rejuvenate mentally.

As a busy entrepreneur that will spend the majority of your time serving others, the simple act of spending time alone can be one of your greatest tools for success.

Taking a break or spending time alone will give you the chance you need to think, sort out the many things going on in your mind, plan and strategize. More importantly the quiet time will offer you the opportunity to receive divine inspiration and be more creative.

It will also leave you feeling energized and better able to deal with the daily going-on's of life and your business.

Boss Note: Communication Really Is The Key

"You cannot be successful in business if you can't communicate what you do or what you have to offer with others."

No matter what type of business you run, communication will take center stage -whether it's verbal, non-verbal, visual or written. You may need to know how to communicate:

- your brand vision with the graphic designer
- the value you deliver to your future customers
- workflow instructions to employees or interns
- the heart of your business to your social media followers
- your pitch, in an email to the blog you want to write about your business
- your product specs with your vendors or contractors

Communication takes all forms; phone calls, pitches, meetings, networking events, sales videos, email newsletters, simply introducing yourself to a stranger ... you get the idea.

If you're too afraid to speak to people, or don't know how to draft an effective email that gets your point across, you're going to be in trouble.

The good news is these skills can be learned. You just need to be willing to learn them and put in the work that's required to grow and improve. Do not allow your inability to communicate as well as you would like to, stop you from moving in the right direction.

Take me for example; I *never* could have imagined that when I would become an author that I'd actually write a book myself. Even though I was challenged by fear and a constant replay of a little lie I'd been telling myself for years regarding my ability to write well or at all, I was able to overcome.

The truth is, anyone can become better at speaking and writing if they practice.

The key to great communication is to stop thinking about yourself. Literally. Put the focus on the people you're communicating with.

For example when you're writing an email asking for something you want, ask yourself, "What would make this person receiving this email, happy? What's in it for them? How can you frame what you're asking as something that solves one of their problems?"

When you're creating the sales page for your product on your website, ask yourself, "What value does the customer receive by buying this product? How does it make their life easier and help them achieve *their* goals and/or ideal life?"

When you're on the phone with the manufacturer who'll make your product, ask yourself, "If I was a manufacturer, how would

I want to receive this information? How can I make it the most clear and organized for him or her?"

"When you anticipate the other person's needs and wants, people will absolutely love to hear from you."

Another way to feel confident about communicating is to find the best way for you to communicate; there are so many media to choose from.

If you like to talk, try video Facebook Live, Instagram Live, Periscope, YouTube or Snapchat.

If the written word is more your thing, start a blog or share on Facebook or Twitter. If you're a more visual person, use visual media like Instagram or Pinterest.

Pick the platform that's best for you and stick to it. Consistency and content go hand in hand.

Boss Note: Investing In Yourself is Investing In Your Business

"Without you, your business doesn't exist, so your mental state, physical health and overall wellbeing should be at the top of your priorities."

Lots of new entrepreneurs get so excited about growing their businesses that they forget to grow themselves. It's very possible for your business' growth to outpace your personal growth.

If this happens, you may find yourself unable to sustain the pace, mental strain and the pressure that come with success.

Think about the moments when you've felt yourself growing spiritually, emotionally, in leadership or in the way you communicate.

What were you doing then? Whom were you around? What kinds of resources were you taking in? Who was supporting you? How did you relax and connect with other people?

When you know the answers to those questions, you can keep yourself in check and in the best position to develop as a human being, making you better equipped to be a strong leader and better business owner - even if you're just leading yourself for now.

I remember having to speak in front of large crowds when my business was starting. At some points I noticed myself out of breath because of my weight at the time. I immediately started to make my health more of a priority than I had in the past and lost a lot of weight. Although I'm not 100 percent where I want to be yet, I've made a conscious effort to be mindful of what I put in my mouth and to nourish my body to the best of my ability most days. I started to think of myself as a company asset. If you're a solopreneur, you're actually your company's most important asset. Take Care Of Yourself!

Think you don't have time to exercise, sleep or eat well? Do you have time to be sick for a month and unable to work? Prevention is the best cure. When your spirit is fed and your body is running at an optimal level, your effectiveness and ability to run your business will also be better.

Boss Note: Take the Time to Gain Clarity

Each time you have the chance to take on something new in your business, whether it's a new product, a new partnership or even a new client, ask yourself, "How does doing this get me closer to my end goal?"

If you want to save yourself time, money and from making bad decisions, ask yourself the question above. If the answer is, "*It doesn't,*" move on so you have the bandwidth to say yes to something that does.

So many new entrepreneurs run around like a chicken with its head cut off.

Doing everything. Saying yes to everything. Trying anything. Entrepreneurs do this when they don't have a clear goal.

Make a plan. Five-year plans are good, but 12-month plans are better. Break your year down into 90-day cycles, each with mini-goals that move you incrementally toward your long-term goals. You'll get more done that way.

Establish a plan of action for each month and each week. Then, focus each day on what you can accomplish *that day*. You'll be able to go to bed satisfied, knowing you put in the work.

Boss Note: Develop Before You Delegate

You need to *know* your business in order to *grow* your business. You can't give direction and be determining what results you want if you don't have some understanding of the task you're thinking about delegating.

Should you decide to hire, it's important to know that a good leader already knows the destination, knows why it's worthwhile to get there and she rallies her workers with specific action steps and encouragement.

In other words, if you're thinking of hiring any form of help for your business, be prepared to make the most of the person's time and energy (and your money!) by knowing exactly where your business is going and why, and knowing how that worker can help you get there.

8
chapter

EXPERIENCE IS THE
BEST TEACHER

Boss Note: All Experiences Are Designed To Teach You Something You Need To Know; Pay Attention

There's a big difference between learning something in theory and learning something as you experience it yourself. Humans have a powerful capacity to memorize information, but learn best through experiences.

Reframe the way you think of mistakes. Instead of thinking you wasted time or screwed everything up, realize that you've eliminated a path that doesn't work, so you don't need to go down it again and you've moved one step closer to the path that *does* work.

Boss Note: Embrace the Tears

"Embrace the fact that you'll stretch and grow. And that you might cry a little. Or a lot. You're becoming a new person during the process."

I like to say that I cried my way through the early stages of entrepreneurship. There were happy tears when I made my first $5,000 and was awarded as the top recruiter. There were frustrated tears as I struggled to learn new skills, tired tears from the late nights and nonstop work, nervous tears when I'd have to speak in front of a group, confused tears when the doubt would creep in.

All those tears represented something. I was shedding an old version of myself and stepping into a new one. I was becoming a boss.

Your 9-to-5 represents a pseudo sense of stability and consistency that's not present in your life as an entrepreneur.

Life as an entrepreneur means you'll experience new challenges almost daily You'll have to acquire new skills. People and things that will throw a wrench in your plans. There'll be unexpected victories, unanticipated failures, and total exhaustion.

After years of up and down I finally figured out that it's all a part of the process. I have to remind myself to embrace the fact that every day will be different.

One day on this journey, you'll wake up and realize you've become a person --and live a life -- that you don't even recognize (in a good way!). You'll do things you never dreamed possible. Crying is just a part of the process to get you there. And that's okay. Crying is good for the soul. It's your body's way of releasing the tension that builds up as you transform into a new, stronger person.

Sad to say, it's the bad days that are going to build character and backbone.

Boss Note: There is No Such Thing as the Right Decision

"You may not always make the right decision, but you have the opportunity to make every decision right."

Decision-making can be hard for us business owners. We don't know what we don't know, and often our decisions are made from a position of lack of experience. Rest assured that even if you make a decision that doesn't turn out the way you want it to, you can be creative and work the circumstances to your favour.

Don't ever let what you think was a bad decision deter you from moving forward. Figure out what you learned from it and keep moving.

And if your bad decision involved or harmed someone you were working with, do what you can to make it right. Apologize, repay what you owe, send a heartfelt letter. Good relationships are the new currency. Do what you can to maintain them.

Boss Note: Do It Yourself

Don't ever get involved in a business you know nothing about and are dependant on someone else to run. You're setting yourself up for failure.

Shortly after the untimely demise of my second network marketing business, I recognized how tired I was getting, how burnt out I felt. I recognized I needed another way to make money, but because I was tired, I was looking for a business I didn't have to be overly involved in - but I made another big mistake.

I had heard that purchasing a dump truck was a great way to earn income somewhat passively, and so I ended up buying one with a partner. There were many problems, but the biggest one was that we couldn't operate the truck ourselves, which meant we were always at the mercy of someone else. Huge no-no.

The series of events that followed the purchase of that dump truck are too many to mention in this book, but trust me when I tell you I will never get involved in a business venture that I can't operate on my own. There are too many variables attached when you have to depend on others.

Don't get me wrong, I'm not saying you should spend all your time running your business by yourself, but you should be able to do most things if you have to.

Never start something because you have the financial means if you also don't intend to be hands on, at least at the beginning.

Boss Note: Don't Coast When Things Start Going Well

"Momentum is gained and maintained based on your movements; you've gotta keep moving."

If you're not careful you can fall in the making-money-can-make-you-lazy trap. It's easy to sit back and enjoy after you've made some money but if you sit back for too long your money will evaporate and you'll have to start over again.

The easiest way to expand your business is to push forward when you already have momentum.

Gaining momentum is like forming a snowball. At first you'll have to work to pack and compress the snowflakes you picked up, adding new snow as the snow you already have in your hand starts to melt, but once you get that ball big enough to start rolling on the ground, it'll grow and you be able to create a bigger ball with more ease and speed.

We can learn a lot from Beyonce on this one. As far as I'm concerned, Queen Bey is the monarch of "ride your momentum and keep it going." She's really never stopped since she got started.

She's been so successful, no one would fault her for taking a break or getting off the grid for a while. Instead she releases one great new project after another, challenging herself creatively and expanding the boundaries of her art and music.

When something goes great in your business, use that momentum to roll forward. For example:

- You just booked your first radio interview talking about your area of expertise. Use that credential to immediately reach out to more stations -that first interview builds your credibility and will open the door for you to reach even more listeners of more stations.

- Your clothing line is featured on a fashion blog. Run a Facebook ad targeted to the blog's audience, linking the new potential customers to your online store.

- You have the most profitable month ever in your coaching business and your clients are seeing dramatic results. Update the services page on your site with some of the testimonials from your successful clients. Or send out an email blast featuring the success stories.

- The online course you launched was even more successful than you hoped. Start thinking now about what you can teach the students of that course next. Will there be a follow-up course? A new coaching package? A mastermind retreat? A way for them to become affiliates and invite their audiences to take your course too?

- You've made your first $100K or even $million. Instead of spending recklessly, start thinking about what you can do, invest in or make next.

Mid-momentum is the perfect time to sit down with yourself or your team and strategize about how to capitalize on the forward motion.

Boss Note: Learn To Rest, But Not Quit, When You Get Tired

Have you ever been on a health kick, going to the gym, eating right, drinking water and consistent - completely on the right path ... you start to lose a little weight, you're looking good and seeing results ... then, for whatever reason, you completely stop what you're doing?

If you've been in this situation, you know exactly what I'm talking about. When you start going to the gym and then you quit, it's the hardest thing to get going again.

Starting over feels even worse than starting the first time. You have to muster up everything inside of you to start again because you now know what's involved.

But what if you had been going to the gym seven days a week, then slowed down to four days a week or three days a week ... or even two or one?

Working from two back to seven would be easier than starting again from zero.

The same thing applies to your business. There will be times when you feel tired. There will be times when you feel like you want to give up. There will be times when you feel like you cannot go on and question your decision to start a business with every fiber of your being.

But that is not the time to quit. That's the time to either push harder or slow down ... but never to stop completely. Please don't quit!

At one point in my career, I had the pleasure of working with one of the world's best network marketers. She was a mentor of sorts at the time.

The network marketing company we were affiliated with opened its first warehouse in Canada. I was ecstatic when I found out this would be happening ...not realizing that this would be the beginning of the end for me and many others.

You see, the company opened a warehouse in hopes of cutting down the cost of shipping and cross-border taxes. But they didn't do their due diligence, and by the time the warehouse opened, is when we all realized that the strict Canadian government did not approve their right to sell and distribute the company's consumables (shakes, nutritional drinks etc.) which were the basis of our business.

If you know anything about network marketing, you know that the real money *is* in the consumables. You make your money on the products that people order over and over again and consume every month. That's where the bulk of earnings and residual income comes from.

With no consumables and the company no longer willing to subsidize the cost of shipping, I found myself with a product (that when imported) I could no longer make a profit on. The cost of shipping coupled with the exchange rate made it almost impossible for me to generate income. People were no longer willing to spend the money it cost to get the products, and the company was no longer willing to help with shipping costs after investing in a warehouse.

Much quicker than I was ready for, my monthly income dropped from $25,000 to $30,000 on a not-so-good month to pretty much nothing.

I remember talking to my mentor about how devastated I was. I was exhausted, burned out and felt like all my hard work was in vain. She listened and completely understood; she was affected in a similar way. But she warned me not to stop. Slow down and take a break, she said, but don't pack up and shut everything down.

She must have been speaking from experience because she was so right.

I didn't fully understand what she meant at the time, but now I understand, "not stopping" didn't mean staying on a sinking ship, it meant slowing down enough to regroup. Taking a step back to figure out next steps. It means giving yourself a transition period to pivot and change your strategy, rather than checking out all together. And let me tell you, check out completely is exactly what I did. Apparently, my stubborn self always has to grow through experiencing everything the hard way.

Each day became a struggle. I fell into what I like to refer to as situational depression. I was mourning the loss of everything I had worked for. I remember feeling like I was on a slide, trying to hold onto the bars at the top like we all did when we were kids. Trying to hold on so my feet didn't hit the sandbox at the bottom.

Trying to climb back up instead of sliding down. But it got to a point that the callouses on my hands became too sore to hold on any longer and I completely let go. That was what my depression, caused by my crumbling career and loss of income, felt like.

If I could do it all over again I would have taken heed to the advice I was given and taken a break … even one for a month. I would have gotten on a plane and headed somewhere warm and come up with a new plan. But I didn't do that. I lost faith. I let the negative things I heard seep into my being and allowed other people's negative energy get the best of me.

Stopping everything completely was probably one of the worst decisions I've ever made in business to date.

A setback in your business is like an injury to an athlete. You need rest. You need a plan for healing. And you need to ease back into work so that you don't lose your muscle and momentum.

When you're totally shaken or experience a huge setback, give yourself a couple days or even a week or month of rest. Work through what happened and how you can move forward, wiser. Ask God to release the hurt and frustration from your spirit so you can focus on the tasks at hand.

My advice to you: when you feel lost and like things are crumbling, slow down and take a break. Take a nap. Take a vacation if you have to. But regroup as soon as possible and get back to work.

We women have a tendency to allow our feelings to get the best of us. But business doesn't care if you're happy, sad, mad, or going through a breakup.

It's important to develop the emotional discipline needed to do what's required as an entrepreneur on a daily basis, regardless of how you feel. The inability to control your emotions is all-around bad for business.

I'll admit, this has always been hard for me. I'm the type who walks around with my feelings on my sleeve (and my face!). I have the tendency to take bad news to heart and lament on things I have no control over for way longer than I should.

But knowing is half the battle and it's something I constantly have to work on. If you're anything like me, it's best to get your feelings in check as soon as possible.

It takes discipline and a lot of effort, because it can feel good to indulge in our anger or sadness or annoyance sometimes.

It's okay to have a break down, a bad day or to cry occasionally, but give yourself a time limit. When time is up, move on. Don't allow yourself to unpack and live there.

Boss Note: Don't Make Decisions When You're Uncertain About Your Situation

"Don't make any permanent decisions on temporary feelings. Feelings fade and storms don't last forever."

Don't feel pressured to make a big move or take on a big project when you're uncertain. Ask yourself, after the feelings pass, will I still be okay with the decision I've made?

Trying to take on new skills and to tap into new aspects of yourself will always be awkward at first, frustrating and sometimes scary. But if you stick to it, the things that take the most effort eventually will become second nature.

All it takes is diligence. One day at a time. One small effort at a time.

When you're facing a crisis or state of confusion, pause. Spend some time alone with yourself and with God. Pray.

One of the most helpful things you can do is to ask for advice from a business owner who's farther along than you are. Ask several if you can. No need to reinvent the wheel. Someone who's not emotional about the situation like you are can help you take an objective look at your business and your life and help you to pave a path forward. Isolation is the devil. Don't feel like you can't share your weak or low points with someone else. We've all been there.

Boss Note: Be Mindful of Those Closest To You

In The *48 Laws of Power*, Robert Greene says, "Be wary of friends — they will betray you more quickly, for they are easily aroused to envy. But hire an enemy and he will be more loyal than a friend, for he has more to prove." Greene says you have more to fear from friends than enemies. If you have no enemies, make a way to find them.

This was another lesson learned the hard way.

I became closer friends with someone I had known for a while, someone my intuition had always told me should be kept at an arm's length. But we started to work closely together and so our friendship also became closer. I thought I had started to see her in a different light, maybe because I ended up being around her almost every day.

Very long story short, I completely let my guard down. I shared and said way too much, and in the end she betrayed me. It was amazing how many people came to me after the fact and told me things that she had did and said behind my back.

Once people realized we no longer spoke, it was almost as if there was a unanimous sigh of relief. People had been waiting for the chance to say things they had been to fearful to mention before. Truth is, I always knew the type of person she was, yet I willingly gave her my trust when really she did nothing to earn it.

Beware of those closest to you. We often give them the ammunition they need to harm us. As you grow as an individual and entrepreneur, you will also find that you grow apart from some of the people you've always known. Evolution requires separation. It's just the way life goes.

Boss Note: You Can't Be a Prophet in Your Own Land

Have you ever heard the phrase, "*A prophet has no honor in his own land?*" Jesus said that.

The people He grew up around thought they knew what He was about and refused to believe He could do miracles. Meanwhile, total strangers who'd had one encounter with Him were dropping everything to follow Him.

This phenomenon happens to so many of us who want to reinvent ourselves or attempt to become business owners or anything more than what we used to be.

The people who love you and know you best can sometimes have the hardest time taking your new venture or the new you seriously.

They may feel that you're not equipped, you're reaching too far or your dream is too big. They may even bring up past failures or throw old mistakes in your face.

Of course, everyone needs a circle of friends to confide in to act as a sounding board. Just go into those conversations knowing it may be hard for some of the people who know you best to see you changing, or to picture you as anything other than the idea they already have in their head. I know how it feels, and these kinds of reactions can hurt.

Watch out for people who distract you from your goals or delay your progress.

Be mindful of people who suck the life out of you or constantly drain your energy.

Beware of friends or significant others who cause you to lose focus and take you off your game. Beware of friends who leave you feeling discouraged after you've just spent time with them.

A true friend helps you become more of who you want to be and encourages you as you do.

If you're single; be mindful of potential partners that don't fully understand why you grind like you do. Don't let anyone make you feel like you're doing too much. The right partner will understand why you're working so hard and find other ways to support you and will never make you feel bad for wanting more.

Boss Note: You May Need to Keep Your Social and Business Circles Separate

Here are some ideas:

- Talk life things with your "Day One" friends and family, and save the endless business discussions for fellow entrepreneurs. This'll save you from getting discouraging comments or hurt feelings it will also help you maintain better relationships with the people you love and keep you from being the girl so consumed with talking business that your old friends start to roll their eyes when you bring it up.

- You need old friends. They know you. You have history. You're there for each other. And you can do your part in those relationships by being the same great friend to them that you've always been, even now as you're changing your life and your focus.

- Let your "Day One" friends know how they can support your new business if they ask, but don't guilt them into supporting you. If you're depending on or get offended when your friends don't support you, you're not ready to be in business.

- Divert friends' "helpful" advice, which may be unwanted. You can direct their helpful energy by asking them to refer friends to you, getting them to help pick your logo or drop off business cards, marketing material or samples at their place of work .

- To talk business, connect with new entrepreneur friends who'll understand what you're working toward.

Boss Note: Find Your Tribe

When all your friends work 9-5s, being an entrepreneur can get lonely.

If you've left the office to work from home, you may literally be alone all day.

But prolonged isolation can cause you to overthink things, screw up your priorities or even cause depression. Find a community of like-minded business owners to connect with - for inspiration, advice and support. You may also have knowledge or expertise that they need too. When you're able to be generous with your experiences and help others, the new connections you make can be fulfilling.

Make the conscious decision to be around other entrepreneurs. Even if their businesses are totally different from yours.

In fact, this is the main reason I've created a supportive, driven community of fellow bosses (and future entrepreneurs) on Facebook and Instagram. It's a space to talk business, get advice and find inspiration where everyone present believes your goals are possible and wants to see you achieve them. Not only that, but they've gone through the same struggles and have found solutions that may help you! You can find us Instagram @mybossisme and Facebook @mybossisme

9
chapter

GET THAT MONEY, HONEY

Boss Note: Making Money is Like Being a Fat Girl on a Diet

Now before you get all offended, know that this analogy came to me as a result of my own experiences -- with dieting and with making money.

Imagine having 100 pounds to lose. I've been there. At first it seems impossible, but you've decided to go for it and you drop your first 5 or 10 pounds. That helps you realize you can lose 20, 40, 60 or even 100 pounds.

Making money is much the same. At first it's going to feel impossible, especially if you've never made any money other than a paycheck before. But if you can make $1,000, you can make $3.000 and if you can make $5,000, you can make $10,000.

The important part is starting to make some, and then figuring out how to make more.

When you know there's a mountain of work ahead of you, it can seem so daunting that you don't even want to start.

Start small. Celebrate the little victories. You build confidence in your ability (to make money) when you see yourself do it and realize what it took to get there. When you set attainable goals - i.e. *"I'm going to make $1,000 with my business this month,"* or, *"This month I want to book my first client,"* you work harder knowing you have set a goal that is realistic and within reach. And accomplishing it will feel so good.

Stay in the game. Keep grinding. Keep making those small but steady strides. Keep delivering great value. The money will come. The person who gives the most, over-delivers and exceeds expectations will always get paid.

Once you're established, think about other ways you can make money. Diversify your income streams. What are some other ways you can serve your customer or client? Think about income streams that can work even when you're not working.

Now that your customers can buy "X" from you, what other needs are they expressing that you can fill?

Boss Note: It's Not About How Much You Make, but How Much You Keep

Making money can be easy, once you get the hang of it. But keeping the money you've made or making that money work for you is a whole other story.

If there's something worthwhile to study and master as a business owner, it's to learn how money works. I believe that "success leaves clues." Study successful people and emulate the steps they took to get there.

Just remember, a lot of people like to pretend they have more money than they do, often to impress people they don't know and who don't care. If you're going to choose someone to imitate, make sure they're the real thing.

There will come times while on this entrepreneurial journey that you'll run out of working capital or find yourself low on cash, let's be real some days you might be flat broke. The struggle out here is real.

If you find yourself in a position where you're struggling financially, my advice is to keep up with your bills the best you can, and use whatever extra money you have to make more money. There's no sense in paying off your bills and getting rid of all your cash flow, only to have no money to make money or invest in your business.

Don't feel shame about doing what you need to do to supplement your income if you have to, even if that means keeping your "day" job or getting another one if you decided to quit.

Boss Note: Make Sure You Have Multiple Streams of Income

Imagine losing your job or seeing your business income drop drastically overnight. It can happen to the best of us and that's why having multiple ways to make money is a crucial part of setting yourself up for financial success as an entrepreneur.

I know this all too well. When the network marketing company I had partnered with crashed and burned, my income dropped seemingly overnight. I have never again relied solely on one stream of income after that.

I always have multiple things on the go and I suggest you do too! If you have a job, start a side business. If you're a service provider, sell products. If you want to diversify your entrepreneurial portfolio, partner with a company that allows you to grow passive income that is inline with your brand. Invest in real estate. Whatever you choose to do, make sure you have money coming in multiple ways each month.

Here is a real-life plan for the different streams that I want to come into my account every month:

- Coaching / Consulting
- Book Sales

- Digital Products
- Passive Residual Income (In Partnership with a Network Marketing Company)
- Products
- Speaking

I also receive occasional income from other coaching-related things such as workshops and masterminds.

Now you need to establish your own income streams. The paper is already printed, you just have to figure out how you're going to get it.

FINAL THOUGHTS

If you're reading these words, it means you've finished the book. Congratulations!

I hope you are inspired and learned a thing or two. I did my best to share as much of my experiences both personal and professional, as I could; to help make your journey a smoother one.

My hope is that you not only read this book and get inspired, but that you also take action.

Knowledge is only powerful when it's applied.

If there is anything I can do to help you, please don't hesitate to reach out and ask.

So Much Love,
Kike-Lola xo

JOIN The My Boss Is Me. MOVEMENT

 @mybossisme   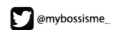 @mybossisme_    @mybossisme

CPSIA information can be obtained
at www.ICGtesting.com
Printed in the USA
LVOW07s2104180817
545570LV00003B/4/P